FINGERPRINTS

THEIR EVOLUTION, SIGNIFICANCE, DISORDERS AND HOMOEOPATHY

DR. RAJNEESH KUMAR SHARMA

Made with ♥ on the Notion Press Platform
www.notionpress.com

To my parents,

whose guidance shaped me!

To my close relatives, whose support nourished me!

To my colleagues and friends, whose encouragement uplifted me!

To Homeopathy, which inspired and immersed me!

And dissolved me completely within its essence!

Contents

Foreword

Dear Dr. Rajneesh, I have been watching your sincerity and dedication towards your studies as well as doing something better for our Science. I am very sure your new effort will help in enriching professional colleagues and future Torch Bearers.

You have been one of my favourite students during your graduation course at State Kanpur Homoeopathic Medical College, Kanpur. I wish you all success in life.

Prof. Dr. V. C. Acharya
State Kanpur Homoeopathic Medical College and Hospital
Director P.G. Education Patna and Allahabad Homoeopathic Medical Colleges
PhD and PG examiner in all Medical Universities in India
Formely- National president- Homoeopathic Medical association of India
10th April, 2024

Preface

In the context of homeopathic principles, we can draw a correlation between individualization and the concept of "like cures like" (similia similibus curentur). Just as fingerprints are unique to each individual, reflecting their specific characteristics, homeopathy recognizes that each person is unique and requires individualized treatment based on their specific symptoms and constitution.

The uniqueness of fingerprints mirrors the fundamental principle of homeopathy, which emphasizes the importance of treating each person holistically, considering their individual symptoms, temperament, and unique expression of illness. Just as no two fingerprints are exactly alike, no two individuals experience disease or require the same remedy in homeopathy.

Furthermore, the use of fingerprints as a tool for identification underscores the importance of precise diagnosis and differentiation in homeopathy. Similarly, homeopathic practitioners strive to identify the unique characteristics and patterns of symptoms exhibited by each patient to select the most appropriate remedy.

In summary, the concept of individualization reflected in fingerprints aligns with the core principles of homeopathy, emphasizing the uniqueness of each person's constitution and the need for personalized treatment based on individual characteristics and symptoms.

Dr. Rajneesh Kumar Sharma

Acknowledgements

I am deeply grateful to my parents and grandparents for fostering my aspirations and supporting me wholeheartedly during my formative years. Their encouragement and belief in my abilities have been instrumental in shaping my journey.

I extend my sincere appreciation to my family, including my colleagues, for their unwavering support throughout my career and during the process of authoring this book. Their encouragement and understanding have been invaluable, and I am truly thankful for their presence in my life.

CHAPTER ONE

FINGERPRINTS, THEIR EVOLUTION, SIGNIFICANCE AND DISORDERS

Definition

The impressions left on objects from the last finger joints are known as fingerprints which are caused by prominent skin features, present on the palm and soles of each person, individualizing him or her out from everyone else in the world.

These characteristics are present in friction ridge skin which leaves behind impressions of their shapes when coming into contact with an object. Using fingerprints to identify individuals has become conventional, and that identification role is a priceless tool worldwide.

CHAPTER TWO

HISTORICAL REVIEW OF FINGERPRINTS

History

- The earliest reference to the fingerprinting of criminals for identification purposes was reported during the reign of Hammurabi (1792-1750 BC) in Babylon.
- Friction ridge skin impressions were used as evidence of an individual's identity in China possibly as early as 300 B.C., in Japan A.D. 702, and in the United States since 1902, and now used worldwide.
- Friction ridge skin was first described by Dr. Nehemiah Grew while the uniqueness of skin was recognized in Europe, by J. C. A. Mayer, a German doctor and anatomist in 1788.
- Faulds was the first to publish the value of friction ridge skin for individualization, especially its use as evidence.
- Kollman was the first to detect the presence and locations of the volar pads on the hands and feet.
- It is recognized that the use of prints on important documents was adopted from the Chinese, where it was used generally, but in India, it was mainly reserved for royalty.

CHAPTER THREE

Evolution and Genetics of Fingerprints

Evolution and genetics

Volar pads are smooth, raised pads on the fingers, palms and feet of fetus due to swelling of mesenchymal tissue, which is a precursor of blood vessels and connective tissues. Around week 10, the volar pads stop growing but the hand continues to grow. As a result, over the next few weeks, the volar pad is absorbed back into the hand. During this critical stage, the first signs of ridges begin to appear on the skin of the volar pads. Volar pads may be high, intermediate or low. The spacing and arrangement of these early ridges is a random process, but it is dictated by the overall geometry and topography of the volar pad.

High volar pad

If the primary ridges appear while the volar pad is still quite pronounced, it is called as a high volar pad and the individual develops a whorl pattern.

Intermediate volar pad

If the primary ridges appear while the volar pad is less pronounced, it is called as intermediate volar pad and the individual develops a loop pattern.

Low volar pad

If the primary ridges appear while the volar pad is nearly absorbed, it is called as low volar pad and the individual develops an arch pattern.

The timing of volar pad regression and primary ridge appearance is genetically linked. Pattern type is influenced by genetic timing inherited from parents. The exact arrangements of the ridges, minutiae and other identifying features, however, are random and not genetically linked. This proves that an individual is more likely to share pattern type with his family members than an unrelated individual, but his identifying finger ridge skin features will always be unique, distinguishing him from any other person.

CHAPTER FOUR

ANATOMY OF FINGERPRINTS

Anatomy

The organ, called as skin, is composed of three layers- epidermis, dermis, and hypodermis. These anatomical layers all together work to provide the body with a defensive barrier, body temperature regulation, sensation, excretion, immunity, a blood reservoir, and synthesis of vitamin D.

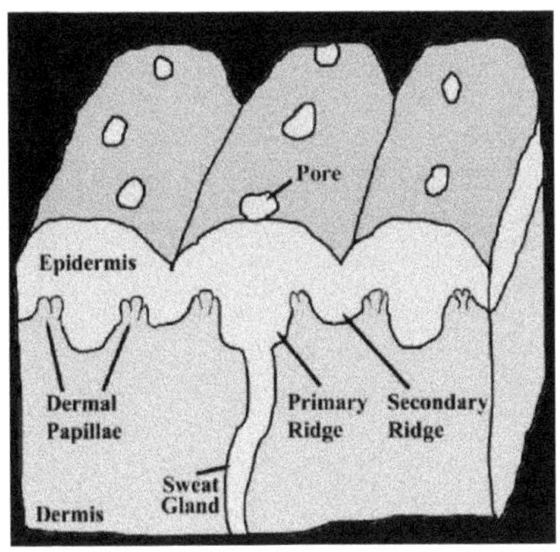

Anatomy of Friction Ridge Skin

Friction ridge skin or FRS includes a sequences of ridges and furrows that provide friction to aid in grasping and avoid slippage.

The ridges and furrows on the surface of the friction ridge skin are firmly rooted in the dermis by primary ridges lying under-the-surface ridges and secondary ridges lying under the valleys. The primary and secondary ridges are interlocked with the dermis to afford support and strength to the friction ridge skin. Furthermore, sweat glands extend from the primary ridges and are fastened in the dermis or hypodermis.

CHAPTER FIVE

PHYSIOLOGY OF FINGERPRINTS

Physiology

The ridges and sweat holes let the hands and feet to grasp surfaces confidently, and the creases permit the skin to flex. Ridges, creases, and mature scars of the friction ridge skin are strong morphological features. Warts, wrinkles, blisters, cuts, and calluses may also appear on the friction ridge skin and are frequently transient morphological features.

Persistence of Friction Ridge skin

It is maintained by following factors-

- Physical attachments throughout the skin
- Regulation of keratinocyte production and differentiation
- Increased cell production in the suprabasal layer of the primary ridges
- Enhanced anchorage of the basal cells in the secondary ridges
- Cell communication

The basal layer of keratinocytes arrange for the pattern for the surface ridges and furrows. Cell communication ensures that basal cell proliferation is stimulated and inhibited in a coordinated manner. As the basal keratinocytes divide, the cell-to-cell attachments ensure that the cells move toward the surface in performance.

The friction ridge skin, although durable, undergoes subtle changes with aging. The organization of the friction ridges does not change; the ridges and furrows maintain their position in the skin. Progressing age has two effects on the friction ridge skin-

- The surface ridges tend to flatten, making them appear “less sharp”
- Loss of elasticity in the dermis causes the skin to become flaccid and to wrinkle.

CHAPTER SIX

TYPES OF FINGERPRINTS

Types

As the skin evolution takes place through the entire process of ridge formation, many factors contribute to the end result like complete structural distinctiveness, from ridge path to ridge shape. Pattern Formation depends on-

Shape of the Volar Pad

It is observed that ridges tend to align perpendicularly to physical compression across a surface.

Symmetrical Volar Pad

If the volar pad and other elements of finger growth are symmetrical during the onset of primary ridge formation, then a symmetrical pattern, a whorl, or an arch will result.

Asymmetrical Volar Pad

The degree of asymmetry of the finger volar pad during the development of the first ridges determines the asymmetry of the pattern type.

Size of the Volar Pad

Pattern Size

The size, chiefly the height, of the volar pad during primary ridge formation disturbs the ridge count from the core to the delta of normal friction ridge patterns.

Timing Events

The ridge count of a friction ridge pattern is related to three different events-

- The timing of the onset of volar pad regression
- The timing of the onset of primary ridge formation
- Late maturers had higher-than-average ridge counts, and early maturers had lower-than-average ridge counts

Differences in the timing of either event will affect the ridge count of that particular pattern-

- Early onset of volar pad regression would lead to a volar pad that was in a more regressed state at the time of the onset of primary ridge formation, and a relatively low-ridge-count pattern or arch would likely result.
- Late onset of volar pad regression would mean that the pad was still relatively large when primary ridges began forming, and a high-ridge-count pattern would more likely result like whorl pattern.

- Normal onset of volar pad regression may lead to two types of ridges formation-
    - Earlier-than-average onset of primary ridge formation on a larger-than-average volar pad, leading to a higher-than-average ridge count
    - Later-than-average onset of primary ridge formation would occur on a smaller-than-average volar pad, leading to a lower-than-average ridge count

Diet and environmental factors

The size of the volar pad with respect to the finger is also affected by many factors. Diet and chemical intake of the mother, hormone levels, radiation levels, and any other factors that affect the growth rate of the fetus during the critical stage could all indirectly affect the ridge counts of the developing friction ridges on the finger. It is important to remember that anything that affects the tension across the surface of the finger could affect the resulting ridge alignment and pattern type.

Delta Placement

The onset of cellular proliferation, which begins primary ridge formation, occurs first in three distinct areas-

- The apex of the volar pad which corresponds to the core of the fingerprint pattern
- The distal periphery, or tip of the finger near the nailbed
- The distal interphalangeal flexion crease area below the delta in a fingerprint

As ridge formation advances, new proliferation occurs on the edges of the current ridge fields in areas that do not yet display primary ridge formation. These three areas of ridges converge as they form, meeting in the delta area of the finger. This wavelike procedure of three converging fields permits for the picturing of how deltas most likely form.

If ridges begin forming on the apex of the pad first and proceed outward before formation begins on the tip and joint areas, then by the time the fields meet, a relatively large distance will have been traversed by the field on the apex of the pad, and a high-count pattern will be formed.

If the ridges form primarily on the two outermost portions and proceed inward, and formation begins at the last instant on the apex of the pad, then only a few ridges may be molded by the time the fields meet, and a very low-count pattern is created.

CHAPTER SEVEN

SIGNIFICANCE OF FINGERPRINTS

Significance

After maturation of the primary and secondary ridges at 24 week's gestational age, anastomoses begin to cross through the dermis, linking primary and secondary ridges and molding the upper portion of the dermis into papillae pegs. Papillae continue to change even into late adulthood and become complex. Although the shape of the epidermal-dermal boundary may change over time, the rate of skin cell production in the basal layer of skin remains the same because changes in the shape of the basal layer sheet do not produce features that appear significantly different on the surface. The consistent rate of basal skin cell proliferation in neighboring areas of skin provides consistent unique detail to the surface of the skin. The pattern increases many times over in size, but the sequence of ridges never changes throughout fetal and adult life, barring injury or disease that affects the basal layer of skin.

The uniqueness of fingerprints mirrors the fundamental principle of homeopathy, which emphasizes the importance of treating each person holistically, considering their symptoms, temperament, and unique expression of illness. Just as no two fingerprints are exactly alike, no two individuals experience disease or require the same remedy in homeopathy.

Uniqueness of fingerprints

The uniqueness of fingerprints may be grouped in three levels and it depends on three main factors.

- Ridge Path
- Ridge Morphology
- Maturation of the Skin

First level uniqueness

The uniqueness of friction skin is due to innumerable haphazard forces. The fetal volar pads play a major role in affecting the tensions that directly influence pattern formation by volar pad symmetry and ridge count by volar pad size.

Second level uniqueness

Localized stresses like tensions and compressions, resulting from the growth of the tissue layers of the digit and interactions with existing ridge fields, create the basics for second-level uniqueness.

Third level uniqueness

Ridge morphology is the surface manifestation of a unique heterogeneous cellular community along the basement membrane, which constantly feeds the epidermis a three-dimensional portrait of its uniqueness. It is completely inconceivable that the physical stresses and cellular distributions that create that community could be exactly duplicated, on any level, in two different areas of developing fetal tissue.

Each section of every ridge is unique. Therefore, any ridge arrangement, regardless of quantity, cannot be replicated. Wide variations in the amount of detail that is recorded from the three-dimensional skin to the two-dimensional impression during any given contact may result in the impossibility of individualization of some latent impressions, but the arrangement of features on the skin and the resulting details in the impression on a surface is still unique.

CHAPTER EIGHT

Disorders related to Fingerprints

Disorders related to fingerprints

The fingerprint disorders may be congenital or acquired along with permanent damage. The congenital form presents with the absence of friction ridges since birth and acquired forms may vary depending on causes.

Congenital disorders

Naegeli-Franceschetti-Jadassohn syndrome (NFJS)

This reticulate pigmentary disorder is a rare autosomal dominant form of ectodermal dysplasia that affects the skin, sweat glands, nails, and teeth and, notably, no fingerprints.

Dermatopathia pigmentosa reticularis (DPR)

It is a rare ectodermal dysplasia with a triad of generalized reticulate hyperpigmentation, non cicatricial alopecia, and onychodystrophy, remarkably, no fingerprints. Above both diseases are believed to arise out of keratin-related gene mutations and cell self-destruction that occurs in the basal layer of skin.

Adermatoglyphia

Adermatoglyphia is an extremely rare genetic disorder that causes a person to have no fingerprints. The patients of adermatoglyphia have no symptoms other than the loss of fingerprints. It is also called an immigration delay disease. A mutation in a particular protein gene, SMACRAD1, plays a critical role in the restoration of heterochromatin organization and propagation of epigenetic patterns. It results in a shortened form of the skin-specific protein. The heterozygous mode of mutation suggests an autosomal dominant mode of inheritance.

Acquired disorders

Temporary damage

Chemotherapy can also temporarily cause loss of fingerprints. Chemotherapy-induced acral erythema causes painful swelling and peeling on the palms of hands and soles of feet and sloughing the fingerprints off with the skin.

In most cases, fingerprints will grow back after exposure to abrasive, caustic, or hot conditions ceases. This regeneration occurs because the imprinting of fingerprints is ingrained in the deeper layers of the skin. Once the skin has healed from any damage caused by these conditions, the unique patterns of the friction ridge skin typically return.

Skin diseases

Several skin diseases may cause alterations in fingerprints because the color of the skin and structure of the epidermis and dermis are influenced.

- Hand eczema
- Pompholyx
- Tinea of the palm or tinea manus
- Pyoderma
- Pitted keratolysis
- Keratolysis exfoliativa
- Lichen planus
- Acanthosis nigricans
- Pyogenic granuloma
- Systemic sclerosis
- Raynaud's phenomenon
- Drug-induced skin reactions
- Leprosy
- Herpes simplex virus
- Scabies
- Erythema multiforme
- Dermatitis artefacta
- Hand, foot, and mouth disease (HFMD)
- Xanthomas
- Carotenosis
- Scarlet fever or scarlatina
- Kawasaki's disease
- Secondary syphilis
- Hereditary hemorrhagic telangiectasia
- Diseases Causing Histopathological Changes in the Junction of Epidermis and Dermis
- Warts or verruca vulgaris
- Psoriasis
- Systemic lupus erythematosus (SLE)
- Epidermolysis bullosa

Permanent Damage

In some cases, damage to a fingertip extends deeply into the skin's generating layer, resulting in permanent changes to the fingerprint as deep burns, mechanical injuries, gangrene, amputation, etc.

Aging

The ridges on fingerprints may become thicker and shorter with advancing age, such that the prints of many elderly people can be difficult to detect.

CHAPTER NINE

FINGERPRINTS AND INDIVIDUALIZATION

Fingerprints and Individualization

In the context of homeopathic principles, we can draw a correlation between individualization and the concept of "like cures like" (similia similibus curentur). Just as fingerprints are unique to each individual, reflecting their specific characteristics, homeopathy recognizes that each person is unique and requires individualized treatment based on their specific symptoms and constitution.

Furthermore, the use of fingerprints as a tool for identification underscores the importance of precise diagnosis and differentiation in homeopathy. Similarly, homeopathic practitioners strive to identify the unique characteristics and patterns of symptoms exhibited by each patient to select the most appropriate remedy.

In summary, the concept of individualization reflected in fingerprints aligns with the core principles of homeopathy, emphasizing the uniqueness of each person's constitution and the need for personalized treatment based on individual characteristics and symptoms.

Eleven patterns appear on fingerprints explaining personality characteristics. Each pattern on each finger may be explained differently with different analyses.

Simple Arch Patterns

Shape

Hill-shaped, curved top, no triangle.

Simple arch

Personality

Hard working, careful, introvert, performs duties without protest, likes to follow the steps, down to earth, do not favor taking risks.

Remedies

acon. adam. aeth. agar. agath-a. aids. alco. allox. aln. Aloe alum-p. alum-sil. alum. am-c. am-m. ambr. Aml-ns. anac. ang. anh. ant-t. apis aq-mar. ara-maca. arg-n. arge-pl. arist-cl. arizon-l. arn. ars-s-f. ARS. asar. atp. aur-ar. aur-i. Aur-m-n. aur-s. AUR. bamb-a. Bar-c. bell. bism. borx. Brass-n-o. brom. bry. bufo but-ac. cact. calc-act. calc-ar. calc-f. calc-p. calc-sil. calc. cann-i. cann-xyz. canth. caps. carb-an. carbn-s. carc. caust. cere-b. cham. chel. chin. chinin-ar. chir-fl. choc. cic. cimic. cina cit-v. clem. cob-n. Cocain. cocc. COFF. coloc. con. crot-c. Cupr. cycl. cygn-be. cypra-eg. des-ac. dicha. dig. dioxi. dream-p. dros. dulc. dys. elaps Eucal. euph. euphr. falco-pe. ferr-ar. ferr-i. ferr-p. ferr. fic-m. fl-ac. galla-q-r. gamb. Gels. granit-m. graph. grat. guaj. guare. haliae-lc. ham. Hell. Helo-s. helo. Helon. hep. hura hydrog. Hyos. hyper. IGN. ignis-alc. ina-i. indg. Iod. ip. irid-met. kali-br. kali-c. kali-n. kali-p. KALI-S. kalm. kola kreos. lac-d. lac-del. lac-e. lac-f. lac-h. lac-leo. lac-lup. Lacer. Lach. lact. lap-la. laur. led. lil-t. lob. loxo-lae. loxo-recl. luna LYC. M-ambo. M-arct. mag-c. mag-m. malus-c. manc. mand. Mang. marb-w. med. melal-alt. menth. meny. merc. mez. moni. mosch. Mur-ac. murx. musca-d. nat-ar. NAT-C. NAT-M. nat-p. nat-s. nat-sil. neon nit-ac. nit-s-d. nux-m. Nux-v. oci-sa. ol-eur. olib-sac. olnd. Op. ozone ped. petr-ra. petr. ph-ac. PHOS. pic-ac. pin-con. pip-m. pisc. plan. Plat. plb. Plut-n. podo. positr. PULS. pycnop-sa. querc-r. rheum rhod. rhus-t. ros-d. Ruta sabad. sabin. Sacch-a. sal-fr. sanguis-s. sarr. sars. sec. seneg. sep. ser-a-c. SIL. Spig. spirae. Spong. squil. Stann. STAPH. Stram. stront-c. sul-ac. sul-i. SULPH. sumb. TARENT. tax-br. tere-la. ther. THUJ. Tritic-vg. TUB. ulm-c. Valer. vanil. verat. verb. viol-o. viol-t. zinc.

Miasmatic analysis

Psora 132%

- Sycosis 90%
- Syphilis 72%
- Tubercular 75%
- Cancerous 73%

Tented Arch Patterns

Shape

Like a camping tent with a sharp tip top.

Tented arch

Personality

Has extreme personality, who can be outgoing, may be welcoming one day and shy the other; it depends on cherish and development during childhood. Not frightened of challenges and obstacles, though sometimes impulsive, but is creative.

Remedies

acon. adam. aesc. agar. agath-a. agn. alco. alum. am-c. ambr. anac. ang. Anh. ant-t. apis ara-maca. arg-n. ars-h. ars. Asar. asc-t. aur. Bell. berb. Bov. Calad. calc-s. Calc. Cann-i. Cann-s. caps. carc. caust. Chin. choc. Coca coff-t. Coff. con. corian-s. crot-c. cub. cupr-act. cupr-ar. cupr. cycl. Dendr-pol. dros. Dulc. falco-pe. ferr-p. fic-m. form. galla-q-r. germ-met. gins. glon. gran. guaj. helo-s. hep. hoit.

hydrog. hyos. Ign. ignis-alc. iod. iodof. irid-met. kali-c. kali-s. lac-ac. lac-del. lac-leo. lac-lup. Lach. lact. loxo-recl. lyc. Lyss. m-arct. MED. merc. mez. muru. nat-c. nitro-o. nux-v. Op. opun-s. ozone pall. pert-vc. petr. Phos. Plat. plut-n. podo. Psil. Puls. raja-s. Rhus-g. sal-fr. sang. sep. sil. spig. spong. squil. staph. stram. sul-ac. Sulph. sumb. symph. tab. tarax. Tarent. ter. tere-la. teucr. thea Ther. tritic-vg. TUB. valer. verat-v. verat. verb. zinc.

Miasmatic analysis

Psora 70%
- Sycosis 53%
- Syphilis 41%
- Tubercular 41%
- Cancerous 45%

Ulnar Loop Patterns

Shape

Looks like a waterfall flowing towards the little finger with triangular points.

Ulnar loop

Personality

Gentle, alert, passive, loves agendas, likes to go with the stream, little self- motivation.

Remedies

abies-c. Acon. adam. agar. agath-a. aids. allox. aln. alum. ambr. amph. anac. androc. anh. ant-c. anthraci. ara-maca. aran. arb-m. arizon-l. ARN. Ars-i. ARS. asar. Aur-m-n. aur. bapt. Bar-c. bell. BORX. bov. Cact. cadm-met. Calad. calc-p. calc-sil. CALC. calen. Cann-i. caps. carb-an. carbn-dox. Carc. Cardios-h. carl. cassia-s. castm. caust. cedr. Chel. chim-m. chin. chir-fl. choc. cic. Cina clem. COCC. Coff. colch. coli. colum-p. con. conin-br. cor-r. corian-s. Croc. Cupr. cycl. cypra-eg. dig. dream-p. eup-a. euph. euphr. Falco-pe. Ferr-p. fic-m. flor-p. fuma-ac. gels. germ-met. haliae-lc. ham. hell. hir. hydr. hydrog. hydroph. hypoth. Ign. Indg. iod. kali-ar. kali-bi. KALI-C. kali-cy. kali-i. kali-n. kali-p. Kali-s. kali-sil. kali-sula. lac-c. lac-e. Lac-h. lac-lup. laur. Lil-t. limen-b-c. limest-b. loxo-lae. loxo-recl. Luna Lup. Lyc. M-arct. Mag-m. manc. mand. mang. melal-alt. mosch. mur-ac. murx. naja nat-ar. nat-c. NAT-M. Nat-s. nat-sil. nauf-helv-li. NIT-AC. Nux-v. ol-eur. oncor-t. op. ph-ac. Phos. plb. podo. positr. propl. PULS. rad-br. RHUS-T. ruta sacch-a. sal-ac. sal-fr. Sep. SIL. Spong. stann. staph. Stram. succ-ac. Sulph. sumb. symph. tamrnd. tax-br. tetox. thal-xyz. Thuj. trios. TRITIC-VG. tub. TUNG-MET. vanad. vanil. Verat. vero-o. viol-o. Zinc.

Miasmatic analysis

Psora 89%
Sycosis 62%

Syphilis 46%
Tubercular 48%
Cancerous 58%

Radial Loop Patterns

Shape

The opposite of ulnar loop, the waterfall flows toward the thumb.

Ulnar loop

Personality

Thinks independently and cleverly, likes to ask and criticize, self-centered, loves to go against the majority.

Remedies

abrot. Acon. act-sp. adam. aeth. aids. alco. aln. Alum. ambr. ANAC. anan. androc. anh. ant-c. ant-t. Apis aq-mar. arag. Arg-n. arizon-l.

arn. ARS. arum-t. aster. aur-ar. aur-m-n. aur-m. Aur-s. aur. bar-c. Bell. borx. bry. bufo cael. calc-p. calc-s. calc. camph. Canth. caps. carc. CAUST. Cham. CHIN. cic. cich. cimic. cina crat. Cupr. cur. cypra-eg. dendr-pol. des-ac. dream-p. Dulc. eric-vg. ferr-ar. ferr. fic-m. fl-ac. gaert. glycyr-g. gran. granit-m. grat. HEP. hippoc-k. hydrog. Hyos. ictod. ign. ignis-alc. ina-i. Iod. irid-met. kali-c. kali-p. kali-s. kola kreos. lac-ac. lac-c. lac-leo. LACH. led. Lil-t. lith-f. Lyc. mag-c. marb-w. Med. MERC. mez. morph. mosch. musca-d. nat-ar. nat-c. Nat-m. neon nicc-met. nicc. nit-ac. NUX-V. ol-eur. Olnd. oncor-t. orot-ac. ozone Pall. par. petr-ra. Petr. phos. plac. PLAT. plb. podo. positr. pseuts-m. Pulx. rad-br. raph. rhus-t. ribo. ruta Sacch. sal-fr. sal-l. sanic. senec. sep. Sil. Sol spong. Staph. staphytox. stram. suis-em. sulfonam. Sulph. Symph. syph. taosc. tere-la. THUJ. Tritic-vg. trom. tub. Vanil. VERAT. vip-a.

Miasmatic analysis

Psora 79%
- Sycosis 61%
- Syphilis 45%
- Tubercular 51%
- Cancerous 53%

Concentric Whorl Patterns

Shape

Lines starting from the center of the small circle, the lines on the fingertip appear to be a complete circle and spread out like concentric circles. with two triangular points.

Enter Caption

Personality

Self-centered, competitive, likes to set goals, laborious, subjective, doesn't like to be controlled.

Remedies

acon. act-sp. alco. aloe alum-sil. Alum. am-c. Anac. anan. androc. anh. Ant-c. apis aq-mar. arg-met. arg-n. arge-pl. arn. ars. asaf. asar. aster. aur-ar. Aur-m-n. Aur-s. AUR. bar-s. bell. berb. bov. brass-n-o. bros-gau. Bry. bufo cact. calc-p. calc-s. Calc. camph. cann-i. cann-s. canth. Caps. carb-an. carbn-s. carc. cassia-f. cassia-s. Caust. Cham. chin. cich. cimic. Cina Cocain. Cocc. Colch. coloc. con. crot-c. crot-h. cupr. cur. cycl. dendr-pol. des-ac. dream-p. dros. Dulc. echi. eric-vg. Ferr. fl-ac. Flav. form. glon. granit-m. graph. grat. hell. helo. Helon. hep. hura hydrog. hyos. ictod. IGN. ignis-alc. ina-i. Iod. irid-met. kali-c. kali-p. kola lac-e. lac-h. lac-leo. Lach. lact. lil-t. lith-f. LYC. marb-w. Med. merc. mez. morph. mosch. mur-ac. nat-ar. Nat-c. Nat-m. nicc-met. nicc. nit-ac. nuph. Nux-m. NUX-V. olnd. op. ozone

Pall. par. petr. phos. plan. PLAT. plb. polys. positr. puls. ran-b. rhus-t. ribo. Sal-fr. sal-l. sars. senec. SEP. Sil. spig. spong. Staph. stram. Sulph. syph. tanac. taosc. tarent. thres-a. thuj. thyr. til. tub. ulm-c. vanad. verat-v. VERAT. vesp. vip.

Miasmatic analysis

Psora 92%
Sycosis 72%
Syphilis 53%
Tubercular 51%
Cancerous 57%

Spiral Whorl Patterns

Shape

A spiral pattern starting from the center and move outward, has two triangular points.

Spiral whirl

Personality

Self-motivated.

Remedies

acon. alum. anac. apis ars. asar. Aur-m-n. aur. bar-s. berb. bov. brass-n-o. calc. camph. cann-i. canth. carb-an. carc. Caust. cina Cocain. cocc. coloc. con. crot-c. crot-h. cupr. cur. cycl. dros. dulc. form. graph. ignis-alc. kali-c. kola lac-e. lac-h. lac-leo. Lach. lil-t. lyc. med. mosch. nat-ar. nat-m. NUX-V. ozone Pall. phos. PLAT. plut-n. polys. puls. ran-b. rhus-t. sars. sil. spig. staph. Sulph. syph. tanac. ulm-c. vanad. vanil. VERAT. vesp. vip.

Miasmatic analysis

Psora 43%
- Sycosis 38%
- Syphilis 27%
- Tubercular 25%
- Cancerous 29%

Press Whorl Patterns

Shape

Similar to the whorl pattern, but the circle turns into a long oval shape, has two triangular points.

Press whorl

Personality

Ambitious, competitive, hates to be defeated, attention to detail, stays on an economy.

Remedies

ambr. ang. anh. apis arg-met. arg-n. arge-pl. ars-s-f. ARS. aur-ar. aur-i. aur. bamb-a. Bar-c. bry. but-ac. calc-sil. calc. canth. carbn-s. carc. cham. chin. chinin-ar. chir-fl. cic. cocc. crot-c. crot-h. cupr. cycl. cypra-eg. Dig. dulc. dys. ferr-ar. ferr-i. ferr-p. ferr. form. galla-q-r. graph. ham. hep. hura hyos. IGN. ignis-alc. iod. ip. kali-c. kali-p. KALI-S. lac-d. lac-del. lac-f. lac-h. lach. lap-la. loxo-lae. loxo-recl. LYC. M-arct. malus-c. med. merc. mez. Mur-ac. musca-d. nat-ar. NAT-C. nat-m. nat-sil. nit-s-d. Nux-v. oci-sa. olib-sac. ozone ph-ac. phos. pin-con. plat. plb. plut-n. podo. positr. PULS. rhus-t. ruta sacch-a. sal-fr. sarr. sec. SEP. ser-a-c. SIL. spig. spirae. Spong. STAPH. Stram. sul-i. SULPH. tax-br. thres-a. THUJ. Tritic-vg. tub.

valer. vanil. verat-v. verat. vesp. vip.

Miasmatic analysis

Psora 67%
Sycosis 48%
Syphilis 41%
Tubercular 47%
Cancerous 46%

Imploding whorl Patterns

Shape

Tai Chi-like patterns in the middle, fenced by multi-layers of circle. (Tai Chi is a type of martial art well known for its defense practices and health benefits and has been considered to be a method of meditation in motion).

Imploding Whorl

Personality

Has an aptitude to complete two tasks at the same time, diverse, self-conscious.

Remedies

abies-c. Acon. adam. aeth. agar. Aids. allox. aln. aloe alum-p. alum-sil. Alum. Alumn. Am-br. am-c. am-caust. Am-m. ambr. Ammc. anac. ang. anh. ant-t. apis Aq-mar. ara-maca. arb-m. arg-met. arg-n. arist-cl. arn. ars-i. ars-s-f. Ars. asar. aur-ar. aur-i. Aur-m-n. Aur-s. AUR. bac. Bamb-a. BAR-C. bar-i. bar-m. bell. boerh-d. Borx. brass-n-o. brom. BRY. bufo calc-act. calc-ar. calc-f. calc-p. calc-s. calc-sil. calc. cann-xyz. canth. caps. carb-an. Carb-v. Carbn-s. carc. carl. Caust. cere-b. cham. Chin. chinin-ar. chir-fl. choc. cic. cimic. cit-v. clem. cob-n. Coca Cocain. cocc. coff. Coli. Con. cortico. croc. crot-c. Crot-h. Cupr. cycl. cygn-be. cypra-eg. cystein-l. daph. dat-m. des-ac. dicha. dig. dream-p. DULC. dys. elaps elec. Eucal. euph. euphr. falco-pe. ferr-p. ferr. fic-m. fl-ac. form. galla-q-r. gamb. gard-j. GELS. germ-met. Graph. guare. haliae-lc. ham. Helo-s. helo. Helon. hep. hydr-ac. hydrog. Hyos. hyper. Ign. ina-i. indg. Iod. ip. irid-met. Kali-ar. kali-bi. kali-br. KALI-C. kali-n. Kali-p. Kali-s. Kali-sil. ketogl-ac. kola kreos. Lac-c. lac-e. lac-h. lac-leo. lac-lup. Lacer. Lach. laur. led. lil-t. loxo-recl. LYC. M-ambo. M-arct. m-aust. mag-c. mag-m. manc. mand. marb-w. Med. melal-alt. meli-xyz. meli. menth. Merc. mez. Moni. mosch. mur-ac. murx. musca-d. naja Nat-ar. NAT-C. Nat-m. nat-p. nat-s. neon nit-ac. nux-v. ol-eur. Op. ped. petr-ra. PETR. PHOS. pic-ac. pieri-b. pin-con. pip-m. pisc. plan. plat. PLB. Plut-n. podo. positr. PULS. querc-r. ran-b. rhod. rhus-g. Rhus-t. ribo. ruta sabad. Sacch-a. sacch. sal-fr. sanguis-s. sars. sec. sel. seneg. SEP. SIL. Spig. Spong. stann. staph. Stram. sul-ac. sul-i. SULPH. syc. symph. tab. TARENT. tax-br. tere-la. ther. thres-a. thuj. Tritic-vg. TUB. Valer. vanil. verat-v. verat. verb. vesp. viol-o. vip. zinc-p. zinc.

Miasmatic analysis

Psora 92%
- Sycosis 91%
- Syphilis 75%
- Tubercular 78%
- Cancerous 79%

Composite Whorl Patterns

Shape

Tai Chi-like pattern without multi-layers or circle surrounding it.

Composite whorl

Personality

Very adaptable, thinks from different viewpoints, makes conclusion based on what the environment is, good communication and coordination skills, but can be unfocussed easily.

Remedies

acon-l. acon. adam. Agath-a. agn. Alum. am-c. aml-ns. anac. ang. Apis arg-met. arizon-l. Arn. aur. Bar-c. bell. berb. bov. bufo Calad. calc. camph. Cann-i. cann-s. canth. caps. carb-ac. carc. caust. Cham. chin. choc. cic. Cocc. colch. con. cortico. Croc. cycl. cystein-l. dream-p. dulc. elaps Falco-pe. gink-b. Graph. guaj. Hell. hep. hydrog. Hyos. ictod. Ign. ignis-alc. irid-met. kali-c. kali-s. Kreos. lach. laur. led. limest-b. lyc. Lyss. m-ambo. m-aust. mag-c. mang. Merc. Mez. mob-ray mosch. nat-c. Nat-m. nit-ac. NUX-M. nux-v. Oena. Ol-an. olnd. Onos. op. petr. ph-ac. phasco-ci. Phos. plat. plb. polys. positr. PULS. ran-b. rhod. rhus-t. ruta sabad. sal-fr. sars. sec. sel. SEP. sil. spig. spong. stann. stram. sul-ac. Sulph. symph. thuj. Tub. vanil. Verat. verb. vesp. viol-o. viol-t. Visc.

Miasmatic analysis

Psora 80%
- Sycosis 63%
- Syphilis 43%
- Tubercular 41%
- Cancerous 46%

Peacock's Eye Patterns

Shape

From the center it looks like a peacock's eyes and lips; the center consists of more than one circle or spiral, the end of each ring is connected in a straight line. It has two triangular points; one further and the other closer to the center.

Peacock eye

Personality

Expressive, highly perceptive, with leadership potentials, artistic.

Remedies

acon. agar. agath-a. aids. alco. allox. alum. ambr. anh. ara-maca. arg-n. arizon-l. ars. bar-c. bell. bov. calc-p. caps. carc. chin. chlam-tr. choc. cimic. Coff. eup-a. euph. falco-pe. Ferr-p. flor-p. haliae-lc. helo-s. hir. hydr. hydrc. hydrog. ign. kali-p. kali-s. lac-del. lac-f. Lac-h. lac-lup. Lach. Limen-b-c. limest-b. Lup. lyc. marb-w. Med. melal-alt. nat-c. nat-p. nat-s. olib-sac. op. orig. ozone PHOS. plac. plb-act. PODO. ruta sacch-a. sal-fr. sil. spong. stann. staph. stram. stront-c. Sulph. thuj. Tritic-vg. Tub. TUNG-MET. ulm-c. vanil.

Miasmatic analysis

Psora 41%

Sycosis 25%
Syphilis 22%
Tubercular 27%
Cancerous 28%

Variant Patterns

Shape

Frequently has a combination of two or more whorls, ulnar loops, or simple arches, with two or more triangle points.

Variant pattern

Personality

Likes to communicate oneself in an exclusive way, which often becomes offensive and creates misunderstandings.

Remedies

Acon. Agar. aids. allox. Aloe Alum. am-c. anac. ang. Anh. ant-c. ant-t. Apis Arg-n. arge-pl. Arn. ars-s-f. ARS. aur-ar. Aur-m-n. aur-s. Aur. Bamb-a. Bar-c. Bell. bora-o. borx. Bov. Bufo calc-ar. calc-s. CALC. camph. Cann-s. Caps. carb-an. Carb-v. carbn-s. CARC. carneg-g. CAUST. cench. cham. Chel. chin. chinin-ar. chlam-tr. Cic. cimic. Cina cinnb. Cocain. Cocc. coff. coli. Coloc. cortico. Croc. crot-h. cupr. Cycl. cystein-l. dros. Dulc. Foll. Germ-met. Granit-m. Graph. ham. Hell. hep. hippoc-k. Hyos. Ign. ignis-alc. IOD. irid-met. kali-br. kali-c. kali-n. Kali-s. Kola lac-ac. Lac-c. lac-e. lac-f. lac-leo. lac-lup. Lach. lap-la. lil-t. limest-b. loxo-recl. LYC. lyss. mag-s. marb-w. Med. melal-alt. Merc. mim-p. myric. nat-c. Nat-m. nit-ac. Nux-m. NUX-V. Pall. pert-vc. PETR. phos. Plat. podo. positr. pseuts-m. Puls. ran-b. rauw. rhod. sacch-a. sanic. Sars. sel. Seneg. Sep. Sil. Spig. Spong. stann. STAPH. Stram. suis-hep. sul-ac. Sulph. Symph. syph. taosc. tarent. teucr. THUJ. TRITIC-VG. TUB. Vanil. Verat. viol-o. viol-t. visc. zinc-p. Zinc.

Miasmatic analysis

Psora 92%
- Sycosis 67%
- Syphilis 54%
- Tubercular 56%
- Cancerous 56%

CHAPTER TEN

REPERTORY OF CONDITIONS AFFCTING FINGERPRINTS

Repertory of conditions affecting fingerprints

Cancer - CACHEXIA, emaciation with cancer - chemotherapy, from alf. ars. CADM-S. chin. hydr. Ip. nux-v. phos. sil.

Cancer - CHEMOTHERAPY, treatments, ailments from Alf. alum. Ars. BISM. Cadm-met. CADM-S. Carc. Chel. chin. chinin-ar. chinin-s. ferr. hydr. IP. merc. nit-ac. Nux-v. phos. plb. sil.

EXTREMITIES - CALLOSITIES, horny – Fingertips Ant-c. pop-cand.

EXTREMITIES - ECCHYMOSES – fingertips allox.

EXTREMITIES - ERUPTIONS - vesicles - bloody serum – fingertips ARS.

EXTREMITIES - FELON, onychia, paronychia - general – traumatic led.

EXTREMITIES - FELON, onychia, paronychia - general – ulcerated alum. am-c. am-m. ant-c. ARS. aur. bar-c. bell. borx. bov.

CALC-F. CALC. caust. chin. CIST. con. GRAPH. HELL. HEP. lach. lyc. MERC. mur-ac. nat-m. NAT-S. NIT-AC. petr. ph-ac. plat. PULS. ran-b. rhus-t. ruta SABAD. sec. sep. SIL. squil. sul-ac. SUL-I. SULPH. TEUCR. thuj.

EXTREMITIES - FELON, onychia, paronychia - Hand, palm lach. Sil. sulph.

EXTREMITIES - FELON, onychia, paronychia - hangnails, from lyc. Nat-m. sulph.

EXTREMITIES - FELON, onychia, paronychia - sloughing, with ANTHRACI. Ars. Carb-ac. Euph. Lach.

GENERALS - CONVALESCENCE; ailments during - chemotherapy; after ant-t. ars. cadm-s. card-m. chel. chin. ferr-p. ip. kali-p. lach. lith-f. lith-m. lith-met. lith-p. lith-s. med. nat-m. nux-v. rad-br. sep. thuj. uncar-tom. x-ray

GENERALS - WEAKNESS - chemotherapy; after kali-p. sep.

MALE SEXUAL SYSTEM - Syphilis - Onychia, paronychia Aethi-m. Ant-c. ars. graph. kali-i. Merc-act. Merc-aur. Merc-br. Merc-c. Merc-cy. Merc-d. Merc-i-f. Merc-i-r. Merc-ns. Merc-p. Merc-pr-r. Merc-tn. Merc.

SKIN - Nails - Inflammation - of pulp arn. calen. Fl-ac. Graph. phos. psor. sars. sil. upa.

Skin - WARTS, skin - situated on, face and hands - nose, fingertips and eyebrows caust.

Bibliography

- Aplastic Anemia: Acquired and Inherited > Clinical Findings Williams Hematology, 9e... The cutaneous findings usually appear after 5 years of age and include reticulated, tan to gray, hyperpigmented and hypopigmented cutaneous macules; alopecia of scalp, eyelashes, and eyebrows; adermatoglyphia (loss of dermal ridges on fingers and toes); hyperkeratosis of palms and soles...
- Chapter 140. Tuberous Sclerosis Complex > Skin Histopathologic Findings Fitzpatrick's Dermatology in General Medicine, 8e... plump, spindle-shaped, or stellate fibroblastic cells in the dermis among increased numbers of dilated vessels (see eFig. 140-8.6). Collagen fibers are oriented in an onionskin pattern around follicles and vessels. The epidermis shows melanocytic hyperplasia and flattening of rete ridges. Periungual...
- Chapter 153. Cutaneous Manifestations of Internal Malignant Disease: Cutaneous Paraneoplastic Syndromes > Familial Cancer Syndromes Fitzpatrick's Dermatology in General Medicine, 8e...) Leukoplakia, nail dystrophy, reticulate pigmentation, alopecia, palmoplantar hyperkeratosis, adermatoglyphia, hyperhidrosis Pancytopenia, various ocular complications, mental retardation, pulmonary complications Cutaneous and mucosal squamous cell carcinoma* Hodgkins lymphoma, gastrointestinal...
- Chapter 165. The Geriatric History and Physical Examination > Pressure Ulcers and the Skin Exam Principles and Practice of Hospital Medicine.... Pressure ulcers observed early in the hospital stay may fall into two major groups: (1) superficial ulcers induced by friction or transient pressure and that usually resolve quickly; and (2) deep ulcers reflecting a sustained, pressure-related ischemic injury to deep layers of the skin and

subcutaneous...

- Chapter 212. Occupational Noneczematous Skin Diseases Due to Biologic, Physical, and Chemical Agents: Introduction > Mechanical Trauma-Induced Skin Disorders Fitzpatrick's Dermatology in General Medicine, 8e... was transferred to work in a storeroom, where he continually handled tools, and was forced to retire because of persistence of the dermatosis with its fissuring and bleeding. The skin may be subjected to friction, pressure, cuts, lacerations, and abrasions in the workplace. Repeated mechanical trauma...
- Chapter 47. Skin as an Organ of Protection > Pathological Skin Barriers: Skin Barrier Function in Dermatoses Fitzpatrick's Dermatology in General Medicine, 8e... by friction or keratin abnormalities Premature infant's skin Ichthyosis, Gaucher's (II), Niemann–Pick (I) A primary barrier abnormality triggers immunologic reactions, but vice versa primary immunological reactions may trigger barrier abnormalities in yet unknown subgroups of the diseases: Atopic...
- Chapter 8. Foot and Ankle Surgery > Keratotic Disorders of the Plantar Skin Current Diagnosis & Treatment in Orthopedics, 5e... Keratotic disorders of the foot usually manifest in plantar callosities and are also called intractable plantar keratosis (ICD-9 700). These occur as a result of friction and increased pressure over bony prominences. Some plantar callosity is normal, but if it becomes excessive, it can be painful...
- Diseases of the Skin > Types of Inflammatory Skin Diseases Pathophysiology of Disease: An Introduction to Clinical Medicine, 7e... infiltrate associated with intercellular epidermal edema (spongiosis) Allergic contact dermatitis (poison oak dermatitis) Psoriasiform dermatitis Inflammatory infiltrate associated with epidermal thickening as a result of elongation of rete ridges Psoriasis Interface dermatitis Cytotoxic...
- Encyclopedia Homoeopathica
- Heritable Disorders of Connective Tissue > EPIDERMOLYSIS BULLOSA (EB) Harrison's Principles of Internal Medicine ... EB

has been defined as the category of heritable disorders involving skin that is specifically characterized by blistering as a result of friction. Using this criterion, it was possible to define subtypes by the ultrastructural layer of skin in which the cleavage and blistering occurred...

- Heritable Disorders of Connective Tissue > EPIDERMOLYSIS BULLOSA (EB) Harrison's Principles of Internal Medicine... EB has been defined as the category of heritable disorders involving skin that is specifically characterized by blistering as a result of friction. Using this criterion, it was possible to define subtypes by the ultrastructural layer of skin in which the cleavage and blistering occurred...
- History Taking and the Medical Record > Skin DeGowin's Diagnostic Examination, 10e... Color, pigmentation, temperature, moisture, eruptions, pruritus, scaling, bruising, bleeding. Hair: Color, texture, abnormal loss or growth, distribution. Nails: Color changes, brittleness, ridging, pitting, curvature.
- Miscellaneous Epidermal Disorders > Skin Lesions Fitzpatrick's Color Atlas and Synopsis of Clinical Dermatology, 7e...) Verrucous and papillomatous growths on the vermillion border of lips. Oral mucosa was velvety with deep furrows of the tongue. (C) Tripe palms. Palmar ridges show maximal accentuation resembling the mucosa of the stomach of a ruminant. All types of AN: Darkening of pigmentation, skin appears dirty...
- Radar 10
- Skin Signs of Hematologic Disease > Skin Lesions Fitzpatrick's Color Atlas and Synopsis of Clinical Dermatology, 7e... Figure 20-13. Langerhans cell histiocytosis: eosinophilic granuloma Solitary, ulcerated nodule with loss of teeth on the gingival ridge near the palate, associated with involvement of the maxillary bone. Lesion was asymptomatic and only when the molars were lost did the patient consult...
- Systemic Sclerosis (Scleroderma) and Related Disorders >

Humoral Autoimmunity Harrison's Principles of Internal Medicine... Centromere proteins lcSSc Digital ischemic ulcers, calcinosis cutis, isolated PAH, overlap syndromes; renal crisis rare RNA polymerase III dcSSc Rapidly progressive skin involvement, tendon friction rubs, joint contractures, GAVE, renal crisis, contemporaneous cancers U3-RNP (fibrillarin...

- Opus 2.0.35

www.ingramcontent.com/pod-product-compliance
Ingram Content Group UK Ltd.
Pitfield, Milton Keynes, MK11 3LW, UK
UKHW062308290726
14090UKWH00018B/943

9 798893 636598